The Brass Tacks Manager

The Brass Tacks Manager

Getting Down to What Really Counts in the Workplace

Pat Kaufman and Cindy Wetmore

MAIN STREET BOOKS

DOUBLEDAY

New York London Toronto Sydney Auckland

A MAIN STREET BOOK
PUBLISHED BY DOUBLEDAY
a division of Bantam Doubleday Dell Publishing Group, Inc.
1540 Broadway, New York, New York 10036

MAIN STREET BOOKS, DOUBLEDAY, and the portrayal of a
building with a tree are trademarks of Doubleday, a division of
Bantam Doubleday Dell Publishing Group, Inc.

This publication is designed to provide accurate and authorita-
tive information with regard to the subject matter covered. It is
sold with the understanding that neither the publisher nor the
authors are engaged in rendering legal or other professional
service regarding the subject matter covered. If legal advice or
other expert assistance is desired, the services of a competent
professional should be sought.

Library of Congress Cataloging-in-Publication Data

Kaufman, Pat.
    The brass tacks manager: getting down to what really counts
in the workplace / Pat Kaufman and Cindy Wetmore.—1st ed.
        p.   cm.
    1. Management—Handbooks, manuals, etc.
I. Wetmore, Cindy.
II. Title.
HD31.K345   1994
658.4—dc20   93-7098
CIP

ISBN 0-385-47055-x
Copyright © 1994 by Pat Kaufman and Cindy Wetmore
All Rights Reserved
Printed in the United States of America
February 1994
First Edition

10 9 8 7 6 5 4 3 2 1

- To Dick: For his creativity, objectivity, tenacity, patience, and love.
- To Jake and Haley: For being very special, for keeping their mom humble, and for their love.

—PAT KAUFMAN

- To Dan: For his support, patience, and love.
- To my father: For my ambition and drive.
- To my mother: For her unconditional love.

—CINDY WETMORE

Contents

Introduction

- Busy, successful people have little time to read long books.
- The high points are what most of us remember anyway.
- This book is small, streamlined, and direct. It is intended to be kept on your desk so it's there when you need it—NOT at home in the stack of when-I-find-time-to-read books.

The Brass Tacks Manager

Anger

The one who angers you controls you.

- It's not the anger, it's how you express it.
- Anger quiets people, builds resentment, and stops information flow.
- Never, never, never lose control.
- Act, don't react.
- Don't kill the messenger.
- Write it out, then tear it up.
- Figure out what your goal is. Will expressing your anger help you reach your goal?
- Follow the "two-minute" warnings (wait at least two minutes before you act):

  - Calm down. (Breathe in calmness and breathe out anger.)
  - Ask: "What could the consequences be if I express my anger?"

2   Anger

 Ask:

  ○ "Will I burn any bridges?"

  ○ "Will my anger get me what I want?"

  ○ "Could this person ever be my boss?"

● See Burnout; Feedback.

Assertiveness

Assertive people let you know where they stand. Aggressive people stand on you.

● Assertiveness is taking ownership for your thoughts, feelings, and actions without blame or apology and accepting others' thoughts, feelings, and actions without blame or judgment.

● Some differences between passive, aggressive, and assertive people:

Passive	Aggressive	Assertive
Shy	Pushy	Forthcoming
Apologetic	Accusative	Clear
Insecure	Forceful	Calm
Afraid	Domineering	Secure
Unsure	Reactive	Active
Guilty	Controlling	Responsive
Quiet	Negative	Positive

- The handshake:
  passive—limp
  aggressive—bone crushing
  assertive—firm

- Eye contact:
  passive—downcast
  aggressive—stare
  assertive—direct

- Walk:
  passive—shoulders slumped
  aggressive—watch out!
  assertive—head up, assured

 Language patterns:
  passive—I'm sorry, I should, I'd better
  aggressive—you should, you'd better, you're not
  assertive—I prefer, I will, let's discuss, I believe,
  in my opinion

- Listening:
  passive—always very quiet
  aggressive—impatient, interrupting
  assertive—interactive, attentive, and responsive

 Talking:
  passive—talk very little
  aggressive—dominate conversations, loud
  assertive—clear and direct

● Response to frustration:
passive—self-blame
aggressive—explode and blame others
assertive—clearly express feelings and frustrations

● Others respond to passive people by ignoring them and to aggressive people by being fearful and angry toward them. People feel that assertive people are approachable.

● Assertiveness—How To: The following are the keys to changing from passive or aggressive to assertive:

  ● Increase self-awareness.

  ● Be willing to change.

  ● Be willing to initiate.

  ● Show a willingness to confront and resolve.

  ● Have a willingness to negotiate.

  ● Demonstrate a willingness to listen to and consider others' opinions.

  ● Be willing to take ownership of your own behavior and point of view.

  ● Be willing to ask others, whose honesty you respect, how you are perceived.

● See Change.

Assertiveness— Barriers to

If you think you can, you can; if you think you can't, you're right.

● The following are barriers to changing from passive or aggressive to assertive:

  ● Putting yourself down.

  ● Apologizing excessively.

  ● Crying at work.

  ● Losing your temper and control.

  ● Acting childlike and helpless.

  ● Giggling nervously or crying excessively.

  ● Poor eye contact, body posture.

  ● Tag phrases such as "you know," "okay?" "kind of."

  ● Excessive perfectionism.

  ● Stubbornness.

- Hedging with comments such as "I might," "maybe," "I guess," "kind of."

- Inability to accept compliments.

- Avoiding conflict or always being a peace-maker.

- Excessive need to please.

- Excessive guilt.

● See Difficult Irritating Persons; Image.

Beating the Blues

Feelings follow actions. Change your actions to change your feelings.

- Do something new.

- Indulge yourself.

- Take a walk.

- Call a friend; talk it out.

- Write down your feelings; keep a journal.

- Exercise.

- Get a massage.

- Read a funny book.

- See a funny movie.

- Watch or do your favorite sport.

- Meditate.

● Have sex with someone who cares about you.

● Eat well; get plenty of rest.

● Get outdoors in fresh air and sunshine.

● See Burnout; Stress; Stress Management.

Body Language

Reading body language is learning to listen with your eyes.

- People believe what they see much more than what they hear.
- Look for incongruities. When words and body language don't match, believe the body language.
- Be aware of what your body is saying.
- Confident body language includes:
    - Taking up space. Arm over chair. Sitting back.
    - Firm handshake.
    - Direct eye contact.
    - Large arm and hand movements.
    - Straight, erect posture.
    - Brisk, assured walk.

● Weak body language includes:

  ● Limp handshake.

  ● Hesitant eye contact.

  ● Slumped body posture.

  ● Excessive or nervous smiling.

  ● Nervous gestures.

● Common body talk:

  ● Crossed arms—defensive, closed.

  ● Sitting on edge of chair—anxious, ready for action.

  ● Head nodding—listening, a signal to go on.

  ● Vigorous head nodding—strong agreement.

  ● Hand over mouth—undecided about what to say.

  ● Rubbing chin—in process of deciding.

  ● Jaw or hand clenching—anger.

  ● Shifting in chair—bored.

  ● Leaning forward—interested, attentive.

  ● Looking up—visualizing ideas.

● Looking around—checking for approval.

● See it. Read it. Believe it.

● See Assertiveness; Image.

Brainstorming

Birth by committee sharply decreases the pain.

- Define a concise subject for the brainstorming focus.

- Set the mood or tone for the topic to be brainstormed. If you're brainstorming for Christmas marketing ideas in July, bring a tree and Christmas music.

- You want out-of-the-box thinking so create an out-of-the-box environment. For example, have your staff dress casually, sit on the floor, everyone wear sneakers, bring Silly Putty, etc.

- Consider inviting an outspoken, creative person from outside your department to bring a fresh perspective.

- Keep the group small (five to eight maximum).

- Try to facilitate, not lead, the discussion.

● Write all ideas down. Ideally write ideas on a flip chart then tape pages up where all of you can see them.

● Suspend judgment. Don't screen or criticize any ideas.

● Focus on solutions. Discourage dwelling on the problem.

● After the session, decide on the most workable ideas and refine them.

● Give the group feedback about the results of the session.

● See Creativity; Meetings.

Burnout

Occurs when you're stressed to the point that motivation is destroyed.

● Signs of burnout are:

  ● Increased isolation, negativity, agitation, physical complaints, or mistakes.

  ● Decreased energy, attention span, or enjoyment.

  ● Uncharacteristic emotionality.

  ● More excuses.

  ● Reduced problem-solving ability.

● Causes of burnout are:

  ● Too much stress for too long.

  ● Powerlessness—that is, having little or no control over what happens.

  ● No-win situations.

  ● Too little to do or repetitive, tedious tasks.

- Multiple conflicting demands.

- Delayed and/or no rewards or recognition.

- Prevent burnout by:

  - Frequent praise and rewards.

  - Practicing good time management skills.

  - Learning to say no.

  - Setting realistic goals and priorities.

  - Taking time out for yourself.

  - Letting go and delegating.

  - Taking one issue, one project, one day at a time.

  - Developing a variety of interests outside of work.

  - Maintaining a good diet and getting sufficient exercise and sleep.

  - Laughing.

- See Goals; Stress; Time-Saving Tips.

Buzzwords

To get into the club, you have to know the passwords.

● Benchmark: A standard of quality to which other things are compared.

● Cross-training: Training employees to do each others' jobs.

● Diversity awareness: Becoming sensitive to, understanding, and valuing the differences (cultural, race, gender, etc.) of people so that each individual's contribution can be maximized.

● Empowerment: The business concept of sharing power, delegating well, and allowing decisions to be made at the lowest level possible in the organization.

● Flextime: A system that allows employees some leeway in deciding their working hours: for example, 7:30 to 4:30 instead of 8:00 to 5:00.

- Mentoring: Establishing a helpful business relationship between a senior and a junior employee to enhance the junior employee's career development.

- Networking: Establishing good business contacts, both within your company and in other organizations and companies.

- Team building: Motivating a group to work as a cohesive unit toward a shared goal.

- TQM: A management philosophy system founded on doing it right the first and every time in the eyes of the customer. Total Quality Management (TQM) focuses on continual product and process assessment and improvement based on solid data and input from empowered and valued employees.

- Value added: An enhancement to an existing product in the eyes of the end consumer.

Change

Change is the greatest constant in one's life.

● Facts about change:

  ● Change is scary.

  ● Resistance to change is normal.

  ● Prior notification of impending change reduces resistance.

  ● Any change, positive or negative, is stressful because it takes more thought and energy.

  ● People value sameness and reliability; however, change sparks creativity.

  ● Even small changes impact the entire system.

  ● Fighting change takes twice as much energy as going with the flow.

  ● If you always do what you always did, you'll always get what you always got.

● How to deal with it:

  ● Focus on one change at a time.

  ● Help employees see what is in it for them and how it will affect them.

  ● Explaining why change is necessary helps employees see the big picture.

  ● Whenever possible, include those key people who will institute the changes in the planning of the changes.

  ● When talking with your people, maximize the positive but don't deny the negatives.

  ● Even the best planned-for change can still stall. Make sure someone is assigned to monitor the change process and remove roadblocks.

  ● Help employees understand that a key to success is flexibility.

● Stages of change/what to expect:

  ● Resistance.

  ● Discomfort, uneasiness.

  ● Assimilation. You start using the skill in one place/situation.

- Behavior transference. For example: As you manage and prioritize your time at work, you'll transfer those time management skills to other aspects of your life.

- Integration. The new skill has become a habit.

- See Stress; Stress Management.

Conflict Resolution

Anytime two people are together, there is room for conflict.

- Define the problem.
  - What's the history?
  - What's the current cause?
  - Who is involved?
  - What's been tried to resolve it?
  - What are the obstacles to resolution?
- Focus on solutions, not on the problem or the person.
  - List three possible options.
  - Look for win-win solutions.
  - Decide on the least explosive option.
- Take action.
  - Bring parties together.
  - Remain calm.

Conflict Re:

- Think, think, think, listen, and th
- Listen, listen, listen, and then talk.
- Define conflict as a mutual probl
  solved, not a win-lose struggle.
- Resist the impulse to take sides.
- Show concern and let employees vent.
- Is this a battle or a war? Assess the consequences.
- Be specific about your expectations after the conflict has been resolved.

- Common pitfalls:

  - Ignoring the conflict; hoping it will go away.
  - Jumping in too impulsively.
  - Taking it personally.
  - Minimizing employees' complaints. If it's a crisis to them, it will soon become a crisis for you.
  - Assuming!

- If all else fails, consider bringing in a mediator.

- See Anger; Listening.

Corporate Culture

Successful companies have a strong, discernible corporate culture that employees can identify with and feel good about.

- Companies are value driven. You need to assess their values.

- Values are basic beliefs about how business is conducted and how employees are treated.

- Things to look at when assessing a company's culture:

  - Company sayings:

    - "We do it right every time."

    - "No one is irreplaceable."

    - "It takes every member of the team to do the job well."

    - "Our employees are our most important asset."

    - "The bottom line is cost effectiveness."

● Rituals and traditions; such as company picnics, watches, retirement dinners, etc.:

  ○ How important are they?

  ○ Who attends?

● Image:

  ○ How offices look.

  ○ How correspondence looks.

  ○ How employees dress.

● Heroes:

  ○ Stories about successful people in the company.

● How are employees treated?

  ○ Benefits.

  ○ Profit sharing.

  ○ Retirement plans.

  ○ Personnel policies.

● Job satisfaction is highest when your values and your company's values mesh.

● See Ethics.

Creativity

Successful people color outside of the lines.

- Three-year-olds are quite creative because they don't know the rules.

- Ask "What if?"

- Suspend judgment.

- See problems as opportunities.

- Capture ideas (even incomplete and silly ones). Write them down and keep them on file.

- Challenge assumptions.

- Let yourself dream.

- Don't listen to negative people.

- Seek out positive people.

- Visualize.

26

● Take risks.

● Break the rules.

● After creating, run your ideas past two or three positive people you respect.

● See Brainstorming.

Customer Service

It's much easier to retain than to gain customers.

● Customers want good products, good quality, a fair price, good value, and to *be* valued.

● The key to good customer service is to be easy and be thrilling:

  ● Easy access.

  ● Easy to buy or check out.

  ● Easy returns, changes, or exchanges.

  ● The customer is thrilled with the experience.

● Do what you promised when you promised.

● First impressions are lasting impressions. You often don't get a second chance. Image counts.

● If you don't pay attention to the customer, eventually the customer won't pay attention to you.

- Indifference is the primary reason customers stop coming.

- Most customers don't tell you they are unhappy, they just walk away.

- Customers vote daily with their pocketbooks on whether or not you will stay in business.

- Never argue with the customer. Explain, listen, apologize, empathize, but NEVER ARGUE.

- NEVER BLAME the customer. The customer is not the enemy. The customer is the lifeblood of your business.

- Think of customer complaints as opportunities to improve. Be grateful and thank customers for taking the time to provide feedback on ways you can improve. Remember, most unhappy customers don't complain, they just don't come back.

- Never take your eye off the ultimate consumer and who in your organization is serving that consumer.

- You are either serving the customer or serving someone who is.

- Whoever serves the ultimate consumer is THE COMPANY in the consumer's eyes.

- Frequently step back, look at, and experience your business from the customer's point of view.

● When serving customers, use their names and listen to their needs and wants. Individualized customer service is the key to good customer service. Everyone wants to feel special.

● Remember, good customer service is not about pleasing customers. It's about thrilling customers! Positive word of mouth is your best advertisement!

● See Sales; Total Quality Management.

Decision Making

Decisions reduce anxiety.

● Not deciding is deciding to do nothing.

● There are no foolproof decisions. An amount of uncertainty is always present.

● All decisions have an element of risk. The most successful people have made the most mistakes and view setbacks as challenges.

● It is better to make the wrong decision once in a while than to appear indecisive.

● It's usually easier to get forgiveness than permission.

● Few decisions are written in stone and can't be modified later with new information and input.

● The majority of decisions should be made quickly. The minority (high-cost, high-visibility) should be made slowly.

● Don't throw good after bad. We learn the most from our mistakes. When you make a mistake, admit it and cut your losses quickly.

● See Assertiveness; Goals.

Delegation

It's not working harder, it's working smarter.
Delegation = working smarter.

- A manager's primary job is to teach and train employees. The primary way to teach and train is through delegation.

- Eleven steps to effective delegation:

  - Clarify and prioritize all activities that need to be done.

  - Determine what you need to handle personally.

  - Determine what you can delegate.

  - Match the task to the appropriate person. (Caution: Don't burn out your favorite employee through overdelegation.)

  - Provide adequate information and the big picture. (Tap into the need to belong.)

  - Grant authority along with responsibility.

33

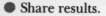 Get agreement and commitment.

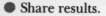 Check for clear understanding of the task.

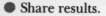 Clarify format and time-line expectations.

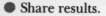 Let the employee know what you want to troubleshoot about.

 Share results.

● The primary deterrent to effective delegation is fear of loss of control.

● Each task delegated will prepare the employee for the next task.

● See Decision Making.

Difficult Irritating Persons (DIPs)

They aren't going to change, that's why they're difficult.

- DIPs:

  - Think of them as Difficult Irritating Persons (DIPs). DIPs in the road are part of life.

  - All successful people have had to work for or with DIPs.

  - Being able to deal with DIPs is a career asset.

- Understanding DIPs:

  - The keys to understanding someone are to understand what they believe in and what they're afraid of.

  - Difficult people are usually scared, lost people. They don't have anything to be for, so they're against.

  - Realize that some people feel so small inside they need to act tall and obnoxious outside.

● People who are controlling are actually terrified of losing control.

● Critical people are usually highly critical of themselves.

● Happy people are nice people; if you're dealing with not-nice people, you can assume they are not happy.

● Strategies for Dealing with DIPs:

● Focus on your response, not their action. We get stuck when we try to change someone else instead of changing our part of the interaction.

● Make a plan for dealing with your DIPs and force yourself to stick to the plan for at least a month. This way your reactions become automatic, thinking reactions, and not knee-jerk, emotional ones.

● Avoid making these difficult people the center of your emotional life.

● Focus on work issues, not personality.

● There are two basic modes for behavior: the THINKING mode and the FEELING mode. Around DIPs, stay in your thinking mode.

● Take "I" positions and not "YOU JERK" positions when talking to DIPs.

● Keep your long-range goals in mind so DIPs don't sidetrack you into hazardous short-term emotionality.

● Don't give DIPs more attention than you give your good employees or coworkers.

● Keep a DIPs LOG. Writing out your frustrations will help you stay calm and focused on the critical issues at hand.

● Ask yourself:
Is it me or does the DIP do it to everyone? Does anyone get along with them? If so, how does that person do it? Would that person's method work for me? Does the DIP have any strengths I could focus on?

● If all else fails, confront: Ask DIPs, for example:

○ What would it take for you to stop criticizing me?

○ What would it take for us to work well together?

○ What would it take for you to enjoy your job?

● Goal-oriented people bounce over DIPs. They don't get stuck in them.

● See Assertiveness; Feedback; Firing; Motivation.

Diversity Awareness

Seeing differences as strengths.

- Diversity awareness is becoming sensitive to, understanding, and valuing the differences (cultural, gender, race, etc.) of people so that each individual's contribution can be maximized.

- Diversity awareness is being aware of and open to an individual's differences without generalizing or stereotyping.

- The first step to working well together is understanding and respecting each other.

- Examine your biases. Look at your humor.

- Actively seek out and pursue situations that expose you to the diverse.

- The reality is that your customers and employees are increasingly diverse.

● Those who succeed in the future will be those who recognize, adapt to, and capitalize on diversity.

● See Corporate Culture; Hiring; Men/Women at Work.

Ethics 41

Is the decision in line with my company's short- and/or long-term goals?

Will I lose a good night's sleep over
this decision? Will I change what I will do
...

Ethics

Your reputation precedes and follows you.

 Questions to ask yourself:

- Is this how the CEO of our company would do it?

- Is this decision in line with my values?

- How could this backfire?

- Am I burning a bridge?

- What is the corporate norm in my business? Is this illegal? Can I live with this?

- Will I worry inordinately about this decision?

- Do I feel okay about telling others about what I decided?

● Is this decision in line with my or my company's short- and long-term goals?

● Will I make a permanent enemy?

● How risky is this, and how much am I willing to risk?

Fast Shots

Brief bull's-eye bullets.

- If you never ask, you never get.
- Decisions reduce anxiety.
- It's easier to get forgiveness than permission.
- Things usually are the way they begin.
- Apologize, don't grovel.
- If you keep doing what you're doing, you'll keep getting what you're getting.
- Successful people have the most behavior options.
- If you're confused, ignore the words and believe the behavior.
- "A" managers hire "A" people.
- "B" managers hire "C" people.
- Negativity is contagious.

The solution is usually the problem. Change solutions.

When office anxiety goes up, focus on the work.

Do your job as if you owned the place.

Catch your employees doing something right.

If they were as good as you, they'd have your job.

● Don't shoot the messenger, or after a while there won't be any messengers; you'll only get "good" news.

● What comes around goes around.

Sometimes doing nothing is doing something.

The laws of success won't work if you don't.

Never complain about a problem unless you have two good ideas about a solution.

Today's employee may be tomorrow's boss.

Enemies do come back to haunt you.

There are two kinds of people, takers and givers.

Yes, the world isn't fair.

● See Suggested Reading.

Feedback

If you can manage to criticize and praise, you can manage.

- Frequent, brief, immediate praise and/or criticism is more effective than infrequent, lengthy, delayed praise or criticism.

- Think of criticism as "helpful advice" to help employees improve and succeed.

- Don't procrastinate. Give immediate feedback at the time the negative situation occurs.

- Focus on the problem and the solution to it, not the person or his or her attitude.

- Ask for and listen to employees' ideas for solutions and improvement.

- Listen at length to an employee's response without defending your position. The employee may need to vent pent-up feelings, and you may learn something you didn't know.

44

- Stay calm. Adjourn your meeting and schedule a follow-up one if either party becomes too upset or agitated to discuss or listen effectively.

- Be clear and specific about what went wrong and your expectations for behavior change. Get your employee to buy into the idea and commit to change.

- Offer support, training, help, and guidance for desired behavior change.

- Major in the majors, not in the minors. Ask yourself, "Is this important or am I nitpicking?"

- Avoid the "but" tendency. For example, "You are great BUT . . ." The "but" negates the compliment so the listener remembers only the negative.

- Always use "I" language. For example, "I think . . ." or "I have observed . . ." Avoid "you" language, such as "You should . . ." or "You better . . ." or "You are . . ." You language causes defensive responses and shuts down the ability to listen.

- Praise in public, criticize in private.

- Have regularly scheduled feedback sessions (quarterly) with *all* employees.

- Have job expectations stated in behavioral terms in the employee's job description. This provides a foundation for feedback discussions.

● The four "Fs" of feedback are:

  ● Factual

  ● Fair

  ● Firm

  ● Follow-up

● If you fail to tell them they are failing as employees, you are failing as a manager.

● See Assertiveness; Listening; Motivation; Performance Appraisals.

Firing

Probably the most difficult job a manager faces.

● When someone needs to go, do it as soon as you can. Tolerance of one poor performer can jeopardize your entire staff's morale.

● Two critical aspects to remember when firing are *documentation* and *confidentiality*.

● The firing process:

  ● Be completely familiar with your company's policies on firing (usually found in the personnel manual) and union requirements. If you have a personnel department, involve it as soon as you realize you have a problem employee.

  ● You will need specific documentation of poor performance over time. Document behavior, not attitude. Also document time, place, and incident.

● Your primary concern is to avoid legal repercussions and assure the firing is done fairly and for clear reasons.

● Use progressive discipline. This includes:

● First: Coach the employee on what the problem is and how to fix it. If the employee claims psychological or drug problems, then he or she may be referred to the company's employee assistance program for rehabilitation.

● Second: Issue a verbal warning to the employee that behavior must improve.

● Third: Prepare a written statement to the employee outlining the problem(s) and solution(s) required.

● Fourth: Set a probationary period with close supervision and documentation. Make it clear that failure to resolve problems could result in termination.

● The actual termination:

● Should be done in person. Consider how angry the employee may be. Do you need to have your supervisor or security present?

- At this point, in many cases it is wise to give the employee the option to resign.

- Be clear with the employee about the terms of the termination. This may include: severance package, outplacement service, what kind of reference to expect, what the publicly stated reason for leaving will be.

- Don't argue with the employee. This is not a time for conflict resolution. If the employee cries, continue the process. If the employee sobs, say you'll leave the room for a few minutes to give him or her time to regain composure.

- Time and place. The preferred time is Friday afternoon. The best location is in a neutral zone such as a conference room.

- Don't forget to get keys, computer passwords, etc.

● Posttermination:

  - After the termination interview, document exactly what was said and agreed to.

  - Decide what and how other employees are going to be told. Confidentiality is critical here.

● If called for a reference, most companies give only dates of employment and position held. This avoids legal problems.

● See Hiring. (Do it right and you'll never have to read this chapter again.)

Getting Along with Your Boss

Your success may depend on his or her success.

- Make sure your boss has no surprises. Keep your boss informed.

- Never go over your boss's head.

- Never disagree with your boss in public.

- Never say anything negative about your boss.

- Make sure you clearly understand your boss's priorities. Plan your time and communication accordingly.

- Analyze your boss's style of management.

  - Does your boss like brief oral reports, written memos, or weekly conferences?

  - Does your boss want you to drop in or make an appointment?

- What are your boss's weaknesses—paperwork, decision making, etc.? Bosses are most critical of employees who display the bosses' own weaknesses.

- Does your boss expect punctuality?

- How flexible is your boss?

- What does your boss value in workers?

- How does your boss want you to solve problems?

- What pressure is your boss under?

- What are your boss's goals?

- Adapt to your boss's style as much as possible.

- See Traits of a Good Employee.

Goals

If you hit a roadblock, find a detour but don't lose sight of your destination.

● Your values determine your goals and your goals determine your priorities.

● Set SMART goals:

  ● Specific

  ● Measurable

  ● Attainable

  ● Realistic

  ● Timely

● Write down your goals. Writing goals down will dramatically increase your likelihood of achieving them. Review your written goals weekly and keep them in view.

● Set both short-term and long-term goals. Make sure your short-term goals are compatible with your long-term goals.

● Limit your number of goals and prioritize them.

● Break down goals into implementable steps. Ask yourself: who, what, when, how, and why not?

● At each step, evaluate your progress and be willing to modify the steps as necessary to achieve the goal.

● Reward yourself at the completion of each step; doing so will help you stay committed to your goals.

● See Change; Success.

Gossip/Rumor/Grapevine

One told + One told + One told = All told!

● NEVER criticize your boss or company in public.
● Facts:
    ● All offices have gossip, grapevines, and rumor mills.
    ● Remember, the grapevine is often an early-warning signal.
    ● A highly active grapevine may indicate employees are:
        ○ Anxious.
        ○ Unhappy.
        ○ Not getting enough solid information.
    ● Pay attention to open/shut doors. If you have an "open door" company and you start seeing lots of shut doors, then there's a lot of gossiping going on.

● Tap in:

   ● Tune in to the office grapevine. Ask several employees what the current rumors are.

   ● When you repeat something, never tell who the source is.

   ● Never gossip about people's personal lives.

   ● If you want information passed on, give it to the biggest grapeviners.

   ● When people share gossip with you, always ask yourself: "Why are they telling me this?"

   ● Tell your employees what you can that's not confidential. To get information, you have to give information.

● Action:

   ● Improve the formal information flow.

   ● Don't take major action to squelch an inaccurate rumor unless you hear it from several sources over time and the rumor might affect company profits or seriously damage someone's career.

   ● Don't waste time trying to find the source. You may get a good idea of who initiated a false rumor, but it's rare to have proof.

   ● Manage by walking around. Ask people if they have any questions.

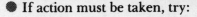

● If action must be taken, try:

  ○ Using someone you trust to squelch the rumor.

  ○ Talking to a small group about the untruth of the rumor.

  ○ As a last resort, issuing a written statement.

● See Information Flow.

Hiring

You are who you hire.

● Before the interview:

 ● Develop a job description that lists all skills necessary to do the job exceptionally well.

 ● Review the job application to match the person with the job skills required.

 ● Develop a list of interviewing questions that elicit skill-specific information.

 ● Check references and read between the lines.

● During the interview:

 ● Gain rapport. Use applicants' names frequently, and ask easy questions first.

 ● Listen more than you talk. Don't let interviewees interview you.

- Briefly describe the job and job expectations.

- Ask open-ended (who, what, when, where, why, and how) instead of closed (yes/no response) questions.

- Good general questions are:

  ○ What would you like me to know about you?

  ○ Why are you leaving your present job?

  ○ Why do you want this job?

  ○ What's most important to you in a job?

- Get skill-specific information. Present a hypothetical situation and ask how the interviewee would handle it. If skills are demonstrable, ask for a demonstration or samples of work.

- Ask value-related questions. For example: Whom do you admire most? Who has most influenced your career? Describe your best and worst work day ever. Who's been your favorite boss and why?

- Some questions it is illegal to ask are:

  ○ Age or when graduated from high school.

  ○ Marital status.

    ○ Religion.

    ○ Race or national origin.

    ○ Children.

    ○ Political beliefs.

    ○ Military branch or discharge status.

  ● Give applicants time to ask questions.

  ● Thank applicants for their time. Let them know when a decision will be made and how they will be informed.

● Deciding:

  ● Select the top two or three applicants and interview them again. Don't hire on one impression.

  ● Don't get caught in the need for a warm body.

  ● Ask yourself: "How would I feel about working for this person?"

  ● Be cautious of the tendency to hire a clone of yourself. Hire for a balanced staff.

  ● Hire from within whenever possible—hire the known rather than the unknown.

  ● Don't ignore your gut feeling. Ask yourself: "Do I like and trust this person?"

● In making your decision, remember, past behavior is the best predictor of future behavior.

● See Interviewing to Get the Job; Listening;
   Traits of a Good Employee.

Humor

TO LAST, . . . LAUGH.

- When in doubt, don't joke.
- Humor relieves tense moments and reduces stress.
- Most successful people have a good sense of humor.
- Know your audience (even if it's only one person).
- Learn your company's "corporate norm" about jokes.
- Never tell an off-color, racist, sexist, or ethnic joke.
- Never make other people the butt of your jokes.
- Humor is funny; sarcasm is angry.

- See Corporate Culture; Stress Management; Suggested Reading.

Image

You never get a second chance to make a first impression.

- There are four key components of your image: dress, voice, body language, and handshake. All four must be strong and consistent to make a positive impression.

- People make their "first-impression" decisions unconsciously within the first ten seconds of meeting.

- An efficient, strong image gives the impression of an efficient, strong person.

- You should perfect your image so that it's not something you have to give conscious thought to. It should be part of you.

- See Image—Body Language; Image—Dress; Image—Handshake; Image—Voice.

63

Image—Body Language

Weak, ineffectual body language can negate all other components of a successful image.

- Posture should be straight and erect but not ramrod.
- Seated posture should take up space.
- Eye contact should be direct but not staring. Staring is aggressive.
- Walk should be confident, head up, and at a moderate pace.
- Smiling, when appropriate, always improves your image.

- See Body Language; Image; Image—Dress; Image—Handshake; Image—Voice.

Image—Dress

You must first look the part in order to get the part.

Always dress for work as if you have an important meeting that day.

Dress for the position you want, not the position you have. If you don't look like you can do the job, you probably won't get the job.

Every company has an unspoken corporate dress code. Know it and dress accordingly.

Pay attention to the dress of the successful people in your company and dress accordingly.

Cleanliness, neatness, and fit are more important than quality and price.

Clothing should never distract from the verbal message you want to communicate.

Shoes should always be polished.

● Women:

- If you frequently get comments on your jewelry, makeup, or perfume, you're probably wearing too much.

- Nails should always be well manicured. If you don't have time to fix chipped nail polish, don't wear any.

- Avoid sleeveless tops.

- Build your wardrobe around classics that don't go out of style.

- Shoes should have closed toes and closed heels. Low to moderate heels are most appropriate. Hose are a must.

- The jacket is the most critical piece of business clothing. It denotes authority.

● Men:

- Navy-blue and dark-gray suits are the most widely accepted colors with solid light-blue or white long-sleeved shirts and a silk tie. Shoes should be black or burgundy and always polished.

- Socks should be midcalf or higher.

- Fingernails should always be well manicured.

● Well-trimmed mustaches are acceptable; beards generally are not.

● Shirts should be crisply ironed.

● See Image; Image—Body Language; Image—Handshake; Image—Voice.

Image—Handshake

Handshakes should be brief and to the point . . . as should you.

- Limp = Passive
  Bonecrusher = Aggressive
  Firm = Assertive

- Offer or extend the handshake. This gives the impression of self-confidence.

- Slightly step into the handshake. Again, this shows more self-confidence than just raising your arm.

- Always make direct eye contact as you shake hands.

- Always offer your name as you extend your hand if there is any possibility the person may not remember your name.

- See Image; Image—Body Language; Image— Dress; Image—Voice.

Image—Voice

How you speak is just as important as what you say.

- You must sound as well as look important.
- Voice is generally a greater problem for women than men. The business world favors deep, strong, low-pitched voices.
- The key aspects of voice (with guidelines) are:
  - Volume—moderately low.
  - Pitch—low. Remember, the higher the pitch, the lower the credibility.
  - Diction—clear.
  - Clarity—always.
  - Speed—moderately fast. (People are more likely to listen.)
  - Expressiveness—very.
  - Tone—congruent with message.

- Avoid: Mumbling, monotone, airiness, and nasal tones.

- Punch important words.

- Keep your hands away from your mouth when talking.

- To improve your voice:

  - Record your voice. That is how you really sound.

  - Ask someone you respect for honest feedback.

  - Speak from your diaphragm, not your nose or throat.

  - When anxious, take deep, slow breaths and breathe in power while breathing out anxiety.

  - Hire a voice coach. Voice is a very difficult thing to change without professional help.

- See Image; Image—Body Language; Image—Dress; Image—Handshake.

Information Flow

To get information, you must give information.

- Respect the chain of command.
- Make sure your superior has no surprises from your area.
- Unless information is confidential, share it. People who feel included are more productive.
- One of your main roles as a manager is keeping those above and below you informed.
- Schedule regular or weekly meetings with all the people who report directly to you. This is an information exchange meeting and can take as little as ten minutes.
- Write it down. For example: "Tell Pat re: meeting Mon." Things that are written are much less likely to be forgotten.
- CYA (cover your backside).
- See Memos/Letters.

Interviewing
to Get the Job

*Do it right with the first company and you won't have to
do it again.*

● Prior to the interview:

  ● Do your homework. Learn as much as possi-
    ble about the company, the job, and the inter-
    viewer. Sources of information include news-
    paper articles, annual reports, the local
    business journal, the local librarian, and
    friends and acquaintances.

  ● Ask for a copy of the job description.

  ● Find out about the dress code. If necessary,
    drive to the company and observe people
    leaving work.

  ● When appropriate, put together a portfolio
    of applicable previous work (proposals, busi-
    ness plans, projects) and take it to the inter-
    view.

  ● Be clear in your mind why you're the best
    candidate for the job.

● During the interview:

   ● Smile and greet the interviewer with a firm handshake and direct eye contact.

   ● Use the interviewer's name frequently. Don't use his or her first name unless you are given permission to do so.

   ● Never malign a prior employer or position.

   ● People like people they perceive to be like themselves. Search for commonalities.

   ● At the first interview, the purpose is to find a job skill fit. Questions about salary and fringe benefits are appropriate only in the final interview.

   ● Clearly demonstrate enthusiasm and a desire to get the job.

   ● An interview should be interactive. Don't dominate all the air time. Know how long the interview will last. Pace your answers for maximum information exchange in the allotted time.

   ● It's important to act as if you want the job. However, to keep yourself calm, remember you are deciding if you want the job too! Both you and the interviewer are assessing "job fit."

   ● Even if you're unsure at this point if you want the position, conclude the interview by clearly asking for the job. Your enthusiasm will be remembered. The interviewer has a gift (the job) to give. He or she wants you to want it.

● Questions you should be prepared to answer:

 ● What would you like me to know about you?

 ● Tell me about yourself.

 ● What are your strengths and weaknesses?

 ● What did you like least and most about your last job and boss?

 ● Why are you looking for a job?

 ● Why do you want this job?

 ● Why do you feel you're the best candidate for this job?

 ● What are your long-term career goals?

 ● Do you have any questions about our company or this job? (*Make sure you do!*)

● When answering questions:

 ● Be positive about yourself and your accomplishments.

 ● Always be honest.

 ● Don't point out problems or weaknesses that aren't brought up.

 ● If a weakness or problem is asked about, be brief and put as positive a spin on it as possible.

● After the interview:

  ● The same day, send a follow-up note that includes:

    ○ A thank-you for the interview.

    ○ A summary of your strengths.

    ○ Why you're the best fit for the job.

● Call back, call back, call back. Pleasant persistence often gets the job.

● See Hiring; Image.

Keeping Up to Date

It's not only who you know, it's what you know.

- Join and attend professional organizations.

- Subscribe to trade-specific journals and magazines.

- Read the business section of your local newspaper.

- Subscribe to your city's business journal.

- Subscribe to *Working Woman* magazine. (Yes, men, you too.)

- Read the *Wall Street Journal*.

- Listen to talk radio.

- Buy motivational/instructional audio tapes for your car.

- Network with people outside of your industry and company.

- Watch CNN.

- See Suggested Reading.

Leaders—Traits of

Lead, follow, or find a new way.

- Visionaries: See the big and future picture.

- Inspire others. Use persuasion to help people see what's in it for them.

- Lead through trust, not intimidation.

- Consider their people their most valuable asset.

- Know that valued workers are productive workers.

- Lead by example.

- Value innovation and creativity.

- See change as opportunity.

- Persist and believe in themselves and their mission.

● Initiate; managers implement.

● Are respected for their expertise.

● See Managers—Good Ones.

Listening

You have two ears and one mouth because you should listen twice as much as you talk.

- Listening is an extremely powerful skill. People will accept your ideas more readily when they feel you have truly listened to them.

- Concentrate and focus your attention solely on the talker. Don't stare.

- It's okay to take brief notes.

- Listen with your eyes and ears. We believe what we see. Is the verbal and nonverbal communication congruent? Listen for what's *not* being said.

- Don't interrupt. Listen to people all the way through to make sure you could repeat their point of view.

- Maintain neutral body language. Avoid grimacing, shaking your head, and other gestures that will stop the talker. Encourage the speaker with head nods, uh-huhs, etc.

● Suspend judgment about the person and issue. New good ideas often come from unexpected places.

● You may want to paraphrase briefly what the speaker has said. Don't mind-read. If needed, ask for clarification.

● Good managers are good learners. You're learning when you're listening.

● See Body Language.

Management by Objectives (MBO)

The objective is to be objective.

- MBO is a management planning and administration tool.
- Supervisors and employees meet to set mutual, specific, realistic, obtainable objectives.
- Objectives are not the process but the measurable, definable results. For example, it's not how many sales calls you make, but how many sales you make.
- Supervisors continually monitor and give feedback to employees on how actual results are measuring up to planned objectives.
- MBO is then used in performance reviews. Evaluation and rewards are based strictly on objective attainment.
- MBO is a top-down objective-setting process. Upper management sets corporate objectives

first; then all individual objectives must support corporate objectives.

● See Performance Appraisals; Total Quality Management.

Managers—Good Ones

Faster than a speeding bullet.

- Praise in public, criticize in private.
- Are even-tempered and slow to anger.
- Listen more than they talk.
- Use the power of expertise often and power of position rarely.
- Are consistent and fair.
- Have a good sense of humor.
- Are well organized.
- Are decisive and open to input.
- Build strong relationships.
- Make expectations clear.
- Practice excellent oral and written communication skills.
- Delegate appropriately.

● Explain why as well as what needs to be done.

● Accept blame and share credit.

● Face and resolve conflict.

● See Leaders—Traits of; Listening; Power.

Meetings

The #1 time waster in business.

- Before calling a meeting, explore alternatives:

  - Can this information be handled without a meeting?

  - Does this require consensus, discussion, or support?

  - Could it be handled with a phone call or memo?

- Purpose of meetings:

  - To brainstorm.

  - To give or exchange information.

  - To make a group decision.

  - To gather support, sell, or persuade.

86

- To motivate or inspire.

- To delegate or divide up responsibilities.

- Planning an effective meeting:

  - Write up and distribute an agenda covering these points:

    - Objective or goal of meeting.

    - Who will attend? There is a tendency to overinvite.

    - Participant preparation required prior to meeting.

    - Key points to be covered, time frames, and person responsible for each portion.

    - Logistics: date, start and stop time, and meeting location.

  - Plan ahead for audiovisual needs and handouts.

  - Determine ideal room setup to complement meeting purpose:

    - Circle: brainstorming, giving or exchanging information.

○ Conference table: decision making, delegating or dividing responsibility, *negotiating*.

○ Classroom: informing, lecturing, motivating, or selling.

● Conducting an effective meeting:

⬤ Start and stop on time. Don't reward tardiness and punish promptness.

⬤ Bring extra copies of the agenda. Having the agenda in front of participants will help the meeting stay on topic and on schedule.

⬤ Stay in control of and stick to the agenda. When topics that are not on the agenda are raised, suggest adding them to the next agenda and move on.

⬤ Review follow-up plans and assignments at the close of the meeting.

● Tips:

⬤ Consider starting at odd times—for example, 8:10 or 9:20. This tends to increase punctuality.

⬤ Don't get caught in the one-hour meeting trap. Would thirty, forty, or fifty minutes do?

● Be prepared when asking for a decision. Identify key support individuals and possible obstacles through one-on-one conversations prior to the formal meeting.

● STOP side conversations by:

○ Saying kindly—"I'd appreciate your input. Is there something you're saying we need to know?"

○ Stop talking and look at talkers. When they stop, you talk.

● See Presentations.

Memos/Letters

Ask yourself: If it were published, would I be proud of it?

- The goal in business writing is to be concise, clear, and powerful.
- Before you write, ask yourself:
  - Why am I writing: to document, inform, ask, persuade, or justify?
  - What is my goal?
  - Who will be reading this?
- Writing tips:
  - Write the way you talk. Use the active voice. For example, "I did," not "It was done by me."
  - Use small, simple words. For example:
    - ○ "house," not "abode"
    - ○ "and," not "in addition to"
    - ○ "ask," not "inquire"

- Use short sentences.
- Be neat and accurate.
- Bullet important lists.
- Use a positive tone as much as possible. For example, say what you *will* do, not what you *won't*.
- Avoid clichés, slang, profanity, and humor.
- Watch what you write. Once it's out of your hands, CONFIDENTIAL is only a request, not an enforceable command. If it's too sensitive, say it, don't write it.
- Don't write in anger. Give yourself overnight to cool off.

- Memo/letter format:
  - Many companies have preferred corporate formats. If yours doesn't, the following is a standard format.
    - State why you are writing. Grab the reader's attention here.
    - State the question, issue, or problem that needs to be addressed or solved.
    - Present the history or background information a reader needs to understand the subject.
    - Propose your ideas and offer suggestions for solutions.

○ Close by recommending the next step or proposing a plan for follow-up.

● After writing, reread and ask:

⬤ Does it flow?

⬤ Are any important questions left unanswered?

⬤ Is the tone as intended?

⬤ Are the spelling and grammar correct? (*You're* spell check can't *due* it all.)

⬤ What are the ramifications of misinterpretation?

● After writing, edit for:

⬤ Brevity.

⬤ Clarity.

⬤ Word clutter.

⬤ Words that are used too frequently.

● Finally, reread the memo/letter as if you were the recipient. If it's a *crucial* memo/letter, have someone else read and critique it before it's sent.

● See Presentations—Effective Writing.

Men/Women at Work

Women are not little men in suits.

- An awareness of how the opposite sex tends to think and react will enhance your ability to be successful.

- The goal is understanding and respecting the differences. Both ways are valuable.

- The following is a list of several different tendencies of the typical man and the typical woman. They are generalizations and obviously do not always hold true. The most successful people are not typical. Their behavior is flexible and has a wide range of options.

  - Conflict:

    ○ Men tend to confront and see confrontation as an arena for welcome competition.

    ○ Women tend to avoid confrontation and prefer to diffuse the situation.

● Decision making:

  ○ Men may seek information but tend to decide alone.

  ○ Women usually prefer the consultative, consensus-building model.

● Mistakes, problems, failure:

  ○ Men tend to blame the situation.

  ○ Women tend to blame themselves.

● Help/advice:

  ○ Men may ask for opinions or points of view but not "help." Men view asking for help directly as a sign of weakness.

  ○ Women ask for it, seek it, and give it; at times, when it has not been asked for.

● Information:

  ○ Men understand that knowledge is power and are quite cautious in what information they share.

  ○ Women share information, sometimes too freely.

● Power:

  ○ Men take and seek it. They see it as a positive.

  ○ Women are more likely to align themselves with power than take it. They tend to share power.

● Praise:

  ○ Men view the absence of criticism as praise.

  ○ Women ask for it, seek it, and give it.

● Relationships:

  ○ Men are self-focused and seek autonomy. They bond by teasing each other and participating in sports together.

  ○ Women are "other" focused and seek connectedness. They bond by sharing intimacies and vulnerabilities.

● Response to criticism:

  ○ Men get angry and view apologizing as unmasculine.

  ○ Women blame themselves and tend to apologize excessively.

● Response to feelings of others:

   ○ Men experience discomfort and maintain a solution-oriented attitude.

   ○ Women tend to be empathetic and listen.

● Style:

   ○ Men are aggressive, competitive, dominating, control-oriented, and want respect.

   ○ Women are nurturing, conciliatory, consensus building, and want to be liked.

● Taking credit:

   ○ Men take it.

   ○ Women tend to share it or give it away.

● Talking:

   ○ Men talk more, make more I statements, interrupt more, compete verbally for air time.

   ○ Women listen more, interrupt less, and ask more questions.

● Questions:

    ○ Men ask how, what, where, why, when, and who.

    ○ Women ask how, what, where, why, when, who, and how do you feel about it.

● Think of a continuum with MALE/MALE at one end and FEMALE/FEMALE at the other end. Most of us fall in the inner 50 percent of the continuum. It's important that we become consciously aware of our reactions and behavior and begin to choose what is best in the situation, not just react instinctively. Our head is on top so it will lead us around.

● Obviously the best management style is a BLENDED MANAGEMENT STYLE.

● See Assertiveness.

Motivation

Feed it what it eats.

- Why motivate?

    - Motivated employees are more productive employees.

    - The first rule of motivation is to have clearly stated expectations.

    - Tolerating poor performance is a demotivator both for the individual and for the group.

    - People are motivated by having their specific needs rewarded.

    - Possible needs are:

        ○ Achievement.

        ○ Affiliation.

        ○ Attention.

        ○ Autonomy.

○ Belonging.

○ Challenge.

○ Consistency.

○ Control.

○ Esteem.

○ Fairness.

○ Involvement.

○ Learning.

○ Money.

○ Power.

○ Recognition.

○ Respect.

○ Responsibility.

○ Security.

○ Self-worth.

○ Status.

● Possible rewards: Remember, different strokes for different folks. To be a reward, it has to be something your employee values.

 ● Tangible rewards are external and generally come *after* doing the job. Examples are:

 ○ Salary.

 ○ Bonuses.

○ Fringe benefits.

○ Awards (pins, plaques, trips).

○ Titles.

○ Status (reserved parking spot, nicer office).

○ Continuing education.

● Intangible rewards are internal and generally come while doing the job. Examples are:

○ Praise.

○ Responsibility.

○ Sharing your vision for your area.

○ Information.

○ Support.

○ Listening.

○ Autonomy.

○ Trust.

○ Input.

○ Feeling needed and that your job is important.

● Motivation doesn't just happen, you have to work at it.

● See Change; Difficult Irritating Persons.

Names and More

Few things are as impressive as someone remembering you.

● Keep a file of note cards or a computer file that lists personal facts about everyone you work for and network with, who works for you, and for your customers, suppliers, and so on.

● Each file entry should contain:

   ● Name.

   ● Spouse's name.

   ● Children's names.

   ● Home address and phone number (for emergencies, sending personal notes, birthday and holiday cards, etc.).

   ● Special interests.

   ● Religious preference.

- Touchy subjects.

- Birthday, anniversary.

- Common interests and friends.

- If these cards contain any sensitive information, keep them in a locked drawer.

- See Names—Remembering.

Names—Remembering

People feel valued when you remember their names.

- When you're introduced, *listen* for the name.
- Repeat the person's name immediately: "Pat, it's nice to meet you."
- Say the name in your mind at least four times while looking at the person.
- If you missed the name or were preoccupied, immediately ask for the name again.
- Use the name at least twice more in the first conversation.
- Write the name down as soon as you have a chance. If you are sitting around a table, write the people's names in the order of seating.
- Make an association in your mind for the first name. The funnier the better; you'll remember it. For example: (Cindy/sin, Pat/chatty patty, Jake/rake, Haley/daily.
- See Names and More.

New in Charge

Being liked is nice; being respected is critical.

- Stop doing what your old job was. Learn to delegate.
- If supervising former peers, deal with that issue head on.
- Go slow. Make no changes until you truly understand the lay of the land.
- Be low key.
- Get clear limits of your authority from your new boss.
- Get to know your new boss's style.
- Ask lots of questions and listen, listen, listen.
- Know you're in a honeymoon stage; everyone is on their best behavior.
- Make no promises and few comments.

- Meet with as many of your supervisees as possible to get their ideas and suggestions and to let them get to know you.

- Manage by walking around; observe, observe, observe.

- Don't let your new "power" go to your head. Cooperation and teamwork get the job done, not your power.

- Assess:

  - What are the problems?

  - What are the strengths?

  - Who are the key employees?

  - Who has informal power among your employees, and how can you get them on your side?

- Make sure you understand:

  - The big picture and where your group fits in.

  - Company values and goals.

  - Company policies.

  - What your boss expects of your group.

  - Your group's history in the organization.

  - What was liked or disliked about your predecessor.

- See Change; Delegation; Listening; Managers—Good Ones.

Office Decor

Cubicles are offices too.

- Decide what you want your office to say about you and decorate accordingly.

- People will make judgments about you based on how your office looks.

- Not decorating says something too.

- Before you "decorate," check out the corporate norm.

- Offices should be arranged to help you achieve maximum performance.

- Decide consciously if you want your office to be inviting or not inviting.

  - Chair(s) empty and inviting or stacked with stuff.

  - A desk between you and empty chairs is a barrier.

106

● Decorate to the next level to which you aspire. Remember, your office is part of your corporate image.

● See Corporate Culture; Image.

Open Door Policy

Control it or it will control you.

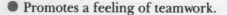

- The *positives* of an open door policy:

  - Encourages early awareness of problems and provides the opportunity to deal with them before they grow.

  - Promotes a feeling of teamwork.

  - Symbolically shows employees you care about them and will listen.

  - Encourages hesitant employees to contribute.

  - Keeps you in touch with the grapevine.

- The *negatives* of an open door policy:

  - Decreases your ability to manage your time.

  - Frequent interruptions decrease productivity.

  - Increases the likelihood of mistakes due to impulsive decision making.

- May encourage dependence. Employees aren't forced to problem solve if you are always available to figure it out.

- Suggestions:

  - Designate and clearly communicate a daily quiet time within your area. Most interruptions come from peers and subordinates.

  - If someone asks if you have a minute and you're really short on time, say "Yes, just a minute" and stand up to have the conversation or say "No, not now, let's set up some time to get together."

  - If all else fails and you need extended quiet time, find a conference room to work in and don't announce your whereabouts.

- Cautions:

  - If you never close your door, on that rare occasion when you do, your department will become temporarily nonfunctional trying to figure out what's going on.

- See Time-Saving Tips; Time Thieves.

Orienting
the New Worker

Things usually are how they begin.

- Be prepared for the new worker's arrival: Have the work area set up, the phone installed, etc.
- Don't leave a new employee on his or her own the first day.
- Assign someone to show the new worker around.
- Assign someone to take the new worker to lunch and generally look out for him or her the first week.
- Much of what the new employee hears the first day will be forgotten. Tell the person it's okay to take notes.
- Clearly state performance expectations within the first few days.
- Orient the new worker to both the formal and the informal unwritten rules.

110

● Make it clear who will be training the employee and whom to go to for guidance.

● Set a time at the end of the week to meet with the new worker and review the week's experiences.

● See Traits of a Good Employee.

Performance Appraisals

To evaluate means to find value in.

● If you've been giving feedback all along, the annual performance appraisal will be much easier. Document and file this feedback as you go along and compile it for the annual review.

● A good performance appraisal is about motivating, not judging. It should be an exchange. Listen more than you talk.

● Avoid last-six-weeks syndrome. Evaluate the entire year's performance.

● Give a written report to the employee prior to the scheduled feedback interview. Be sure to focus on behaviors, not attitudes. Be specific, give examples.

● Rehearse the difficult things to say so you will be as tactful as possible.

112

● When you meet with the employee, stress his or her strengths and make plans to correct weaknesses. Set goals for next year. Finish the session on a confident note about the employee's abilities.

● If there is any reason to think this employee may be fired in the future, be very careful when you do the review. The tendency is to be over-positive.

● Remember, your goal is to motivate your employee. Be clear about your assessment of his or her strengths and weaknesses and help to set measurable goals for the next year.

● See Feedback; Goals; Listening; Management by Objectives; Motivation.

Power

Real power is gained, not given.

- Power is the ability to influence others and outcomes.

- There are two kinds of power: formal (positional) and informal (personal). Usually you must first have personal power to obtain positional power.

- Formal power is your position or title within the organization. Using this formal, positional power is the least effective way to get things done.

- Key ingredients to personal power are:

  - Expertise and knowledge.

  - Associating with powerful people and acting like them.

  - Being decisive.

● Risk taking.

● Having a powerful image.

● Powerful body language:

  ○ Walk assertively.

  ○ Stand straight.

  ○ Make eye contact.

  ○ Shake hands firmly.

  ○ Take up space.

● Indicators of power:

  ● Title.

  ● Office.

  ● Access to people and information.

  ● Assignment to special tasks and projects.

  ● Respect from others.

  ● Opinion sought after.

● Warning: Don't be fooled by titles. Secretaries frequently possess a great deal of power. To be powerful, you must have allies at all levels in the organization and network well.

● See Assertiveness; Image.

Presentations—Before

Know much more than you'll ever say.

● Ask yourself the following questions.

  ● What is the purpose of this presentation?

    ○ To instruct?
    ○ To inform?
    ○ To entertain?
    ○ To inspire?
    ○ To persuade?
    ○ To sell?

  ● Who is my audience and why are they here?

    ○ Male/female/both?
    ○ Old/young?
    ○ Voluntary/required attendance?
    ○ Superiors/peers/subordinates?

○ What is their previous knowledge and/or attitude toward the subject?

○ Are there any big issues going on in this group that I should know about?

● What questions might arise?

● How large will the group be?

● When and where will I be making this presentation?

○ FORMAL/INFORMAL SETTING?

○ Before or after other speakers?

○ Morning, afternoon, evening?

● How can I personalize the information to this audience and their interests?

● See Presentations—Effective Writing; Presentations—Giving; Presentations—Reducing Anxiety; Presentations—Tips.

Presentations—
Effective Writing

Let the ideas flow; then channel the flow.

● Know the answers to the questions posed in the Presentations—Preparing section before you start to write.

● Write all the points you want to cover on 3 by 5 cards, including jokes, stories, quotes, and facts. Use one card for each point. Once all the information is on 3 by 5 cards, organize the cards and the flow of the speech.

● The three Ts of speaking are:

● Tell them what you're going to tell them.
● Tell them.
● Tell them what you told them.

● Write in "flex" sections that you can add or delete depending on whether you are ahead of or behind schedule. (Your audience won't know the difference.)

118

- Write in the active first person—the conversational spoken word, not the written word.

- The adult attention span is twenty minutes. Change your topic or pace every twenty minutes.

- Use humor only if it is relevant and you are good at it.

- Plan to use visual reinforcement of your message's key points. Use slides, video, flip charts, or overheads.

- Close with a BANG—a quote, a call to action, a memorable story, or a brief strong synopsis of key points.

- See Presentations—Before; Presentations—Giving; Presentations—Reducing Anxiety; Presentations—Tips.

Presentations—Giving

Don't speak to them, talk to them.

- Immediately establish eye contact with the audience and smile.
- Speak at a fairly rapid pace to keep the audience's attention. People speak at about 125 words per minute but have the ability to listen at a rate of 500 to 700 words per minute.
- Use the podium as a base of power, authority, and control, not as a crutch to hide behind or lean on. Move away from the podium to warm up your audience or make the presentation more informal. Go back to the podium to regain control.
- Punch your words. Vary your voice, tone, and pace.
- Speak only after you have established eye contact with an audience participant. This will eliminate ahs, uhs, and nervous nonwords and help you avoid the swivel head syndrome.

● Physically move from time to time but don't pace.

● Use gestures. Be animated. Gestures should match the size of the audience. The larger the audience, the larger the gestures.

● Signal the close. Say "in closing . . ." or "to sum up . . ."

● If you ask for questions and there are none, have one closing thought prepared so you can formally close on a positive note and won't be left hanging.

● Be enthusiastic. Do anything, but don't be boring.

● See Presentations—Before; Presentations—Effective Writing; Presentations—Reducing Anxiety; Presentations—Tips.

Presentations— Reducing Anxiety

Push past the fear. Go for it!

● Before the presentation:

  ● PREPARE, PREPARE, PREPARE.

  ● Know much more than you'll ever say.

  ● Memorize the first and last two minutes of your presentation.

  ● Audio- or videotape your practice presentation and watch it. It will increase your confidence. You're better than you imagine.

  ● Arrive early and mingle with the audience as they arrive.

  ● Check out the room setup, audiovisual equipment, lighting, and temperature. Minimize the opportunity for surprises.

  ● In the few minutes before you go on:

    ○ Breathe in calmness, breathe out anxiety.

    ○ Yawn.

122

Visualize your audience enthusiastically responding.

   ○ Remember, your audience is there to hear the message, not stare at you. Focus on the message.

   ○ Pace if you need to. Your body may need to move.

● PRACTICE, PRACTICE, PRACTICE.

● During the presentation:

   ● Remember to smile. It relaxes you and the audience.

   ● Pick out three or four friendly faces in the audience and look at them when you're speaking.

   ● Holding notes in your hand while you speak is acceptable.

   ● If your audiovisual equipment fails, turn it off and go on. Work on it during a break.

   ● Don't read your speech. If a word-for-word text makes you feel comfortable, keep it on the podium.

● Handling hostile questions:

   ● Repeat or paraphrase questions in a more positive way. This gives you time to think.

   ● As you respond, gradually shift your body

language and eye contact away from the hostile questioner.

● Continue on with the next point in presentation.

● See Presentations—Before; Presentations—Effective Writing; Presentations—Giving; Presentations—Tips.

Presentations—Tips

The more you speak, the better you'll be.

- Start and stop on time. Don't reward tardiness and punish promptness.

- Keep the room cool.

- Don't apologize or make excuses. It decreases credibility and brings the problem to the top of the participants' minds.

- Never say "before we take a break." You'll lose your audience.

- Audiovisual aids dramatically increase retention.

- Don't give handouts prior to your presentation.

- See Presentations—Before; Presentations—Effective Writing; Presentations—Giving; Presentations—Reducing Anxiety.

Profanity

You're d_____ if you do and you're d_____ if you don't.

- General rule: Don't use profanity.
- If you don't use profanity, skip this chapter and try to be tolerant of others' use.
- If you do:
  - Be aware of whom you're talking to and who's listening.
  - Be aware of "acceptable" words in your company.
  - Never, never write a profanity.
- See Corporate Culture.

Project Management

These skills are needed whether you're organizing the office Christmas party or putting a man on the moon.

- Have a clearly defined project description that outlines goals, budget, and time line.
- Divide the project into tasks.
- Identify skills needed for each task.
- Identify people who have those skills and get them assigned to your project.
- As a project manager, you are frequently dealing with people you have no authority over, so your priority at this stage is team building.
- Develop a time line or flow chart with critical milestone points that allow course corrections or revisions; build in slush time at critical points.
- Break the budget down by tasks.
- Continually keep the project team aware of the big picture and how the project is proceeding.

● State emphatically to team members that you want to be informed immediately if any task is not proceeding according to schedule or budget.

● Make yourself available to help when problems come up. Don't shoot the messenger or after a while there won't be any more messengers; they will come to you only with good news information.

● Continually monitor project progress.

● Remember, as project manager, if all else fails, you need to be prepared to do it yourself.

● Celebrate project completion with the entire team.

● See Managers—Good Ones; Teamwork.

Promotions—How Never to Get One

Do the wrong things at the right times.

● Worry more about getting your next promotion than you do about your current position.

● Be a complainer.

● Be an eight-to-fiver.

● Be very moody and let it show.

● Fail to respect hierarchy.

● Don't adapt to your bosses' style.

● Dress differently from the rest of the employees.

● Talk about your personal problems too much at work.

● Say "That's not my job" frequently.

● Frequently criticize your boss or company in public.

● Highlight your deficiencies and weaknesses.

- Act indecisively; use "maybe," "I'll try," and similar words a lot.

- Whine a lot.

- Refuse to be a team player.

- Talk much more than you listen.

- See Difficult Irritating Persons; Firing.

Sales

Sincerely <u>A</u>sk, <u>L</u>isten, <u>E</u>nhance = <u>S</u>old.

- Everyone is selling something: products, services, beliefs, thoughts, information. We're all trying to get someone to "buy" or "buy into."

- Think "as if" you and the consumer are a team trying to meet the consumer's goals with your products.

- Sincerely:

  - Make your customers feel special.

  - Find common ground. People are most comfortable with people like themselves; they like to buy from someone they perceive they have something in common with.

  - Establish trust. Honesty builds trust.

  - Use the customer's name and personalize the conversation.

● AT THIS POINT, don't mention the product. Your goal here is to make the consumer comfortable with you.

● Ask:

● Ask open-ended questions: who, what, when, where, why, and how?

● You're helping people make decisions. Find out what information they need to make a "buy" decision.

● Discover the unmet needs/wants your product will fill.

● AT THIS POINT, your primary goal is to learn about the consumer's specific needs/wants so you can determine which specific product you're going to present to him or her.

● Listen:

● Listen for what the buyer wants to know instead of focusing on what you want to tell him or her.

● Listen for key themes. What major factor does the buy decision hinge on? Examples of stated themes might be price, service, quality, exclusivity, durability, and reliability.

- Listen for the hidden agenda. What does your customer want emotionally? For example: to look better, peace of mind, prestige, a great deal?

- If more than one person is involved, listen for who will make the final buy decision.

- AT THIS POINT, you should clearly know what the customer wants, why he or she wants it, and therefore how to present it best.

- Enhance:

  - Present features and benefits of the product so it matches the consumer's needs and wants.

  - Enthusiastically demonstrate a love of your product and a belief in yourself.

  - Anticipate questions and objectives and have the answers ready. Complete knowledge of both your product and your competitor's product is critical here.

  - At any point in this process, the sale may be made. Listen for buying signals. Don't oversell.

  - AT THIS POINT, ask for the sale.

- Sold:

  - Ask for the sale.

● A key to closing sales is to be persistent but not pushy. It's not unusual to ask for the sale three to four times before the consumer makes a buy decision.

● If you get a NO, go back to ASK and LISTEN and gather more information.

● The *Brass Tacks Manager*'s method of selling is the *SALES* method.

● <u>S</u>incerely <u>A</u>sk, <u>L</u>isten, <u>E</u>nhance = <u>S</u>old.

● <u>S</u>elling is <u>A</u>bout <u>L</u>etting <u>E</u>veryone <u>S</u>ucceed.

● See Customer Service.

Sexual Harassment

The less said the better!

- The Equal Employment Opportunities Commission (EEOC) defines sexual harassment as *"unwelcome sexual advances, requests for sexual favors and other verbal or physical conduct of a sexual nature"* when it is implied that failure to comply or tolerate the situation may jeopardize the employee's job status.

- If you are sexually harassed at work, you need to make it quite clear to the harasser that the advances are *unwelcome*.

- Make it clear to the harasser that if you are harassed again, you plan to report it to your boss and the harasser's boss.

- Keep a log of comments and incidents with times documented.

- You can do one or all of the following:

135

- Report to supervisors.

- File a formal company complaint.

- File a claim with the EEOC.

● If an employee reports sexual harassment to you, act immediately.

● Ask the employee and document who harassed him or her, what happened, when it happened, whether it happened before, and what the employee would like you to do about it. Follow all company policies and report the situation to your supervisor and the personnel department.

● Avoid sexual harassment charges by following these guidelines:

  ● Never touch an employee.

  ● Never tell dirty jokes.

  ● Ignore seductiveness from your employees.

  ● Don't use such terms as "honey," "sweetie," "sugar."

  ● Don't have "dirty" books or pictures at the office.

  ● Don't talk about sex at the office.

  ● Don't make comments about an employee's appearance.

● See Image.

Smoking

Warning: Smoking may be hazardous to your career's health.

● If you smoke:

  ● In the 1990s, it's best to be a closet smoker.

  ● Smoking is now seen as a character flaw. People may draw negative conclusions about you based only on the fact that you smoke.

  ● Never smoke with a client unless you know he or she smokes. If the client does, go ahead and smoke; smoking together increases rapport.

● If employees smoke, never state your personal opinion about smoking. If necessary, refer to company policy but stay out of this emotionally charged battleground.

● See Image.

Stress

Don't worry, be happy.

- Facts:
  - Stress is normal.
  - Stress is contagious.
  - Stress is increasing.
- Four basic responses to stress:
  - Resist.
  - Avoid.
  - Confront.
  - Adapt.
- Four common events that cause stress:
  - Loss of control.
  - Change (positive and negative).
  - Feeling threatened.
  - Unrealized expectations.
- See Burnout.

138

Stress Management

It's not the stress. It's how you handle it.

- Six steps to letting go:

  - What things *must* I do?

  - What should I do but others could do?

  - What could I do but others should do?

  - What must others do?

  - What doesn't need to be done at all?

  - Ask yourself: "If all else fails, is it worth dying for?"

    STRESS KILLS!!

- Ten ways to deal with stress:

  - Change the situation.

  - Change your response to the situation.

- Ask yourself: "What can I control? What's out of my control?"

- Delegate.

- Call "time out."

- Choose conflicts carefully.

- Practice positive self-talk.

- Talk it out.

- Learn to say no.

- Practice good habits in diet, exercise, etc.

● See Assertiveness; Burnout; Conflict Resolution.

Success

Success is reaching your goals while living within your value system.

- Successful people maximize their strengths and minimize their weaknesses.
- Successful people see opportunity where others see obstacles.
- Successful people:
  - Are risk takers and enjoy a challenge.
  - Are flexible and creative.
  - Are decisive and tenacious.
  - See mistakes as learning experiences. Win one, lose one, next one.
  - Write down their goals and stick to them.
  - Are curious and constantly learning.
  - Are highly capable in their field.
  - Have excellent written and oral communication skills.

- See the "big picture" while attending to the details.

- Accept and use feedback to improve themselves.

- Are self-confident and use positive self-talk.

- Have a good sense of humor.

- Balance their lives and give themselves time for fun.

- Are energetic and enthusiastic.

- Surround themselves with positive, successful people.

- Are visible and present themselves well.

- Are psychologically resilient.

- The more you have of the above qualities, the more successful you'll be. No one has them all.

- Luck is a factor in success. However, successful people know how to maximize their good luck.

- See Goals; Image; Promotions—How Never to Get One.

Suggested Reading

To keep current, we suggest you read all the time.

- The following is a brief list of our recent personal favorites.
  - *Claw Your Way to the Top: How to Become the Head of a Major Corporation in Roughly a Week* by David Barry.
  - All of *The One Minute Manager* books by Ken Blanchard and Spencer Johnson.
  - *Quality Is Free: The Art of Making Quality Certain* by Phillip Crosby.
  - *The Seven Habits of Highly Effective People* by Stephen Covey.
  - *Smart Moves* by Sam Deep and Lyle Sussman.
  - *Swim with the Sharks Without Being Eaten Alive* by Harvey Mackay.
  - *Working Woman* magazine.

- See Keeping Up to Date.

Teamwork

Picture the Clydesdales. Now picture walking six dogs simultaneously. The benefits of teamwork are obvious.

● Excellent teams:

  ● Start with a clearly defined mission statement that is shared by all team members. All decisions and plans relate directly back to that mission statement.

  ● Focus on work product and not personalities.

  ● Are both goal and process oriented.

  ● Discourage turf battles.

  ● Focus on the goal and not personal glory.

  ● Meet frequently and identify as a team.

  ● Resolve conflicts openly and quickly.

  ● Have an open flow of information.

  ● Discourage secrecy.

  ● Focus on solutions, not blame.

144

- Don't vote; build consensus.

- Celebrate successes and evaluate their failures.

● Excellent team leaders:

- Share information freely, not just the what but the why.

- Are honest.

- Give both praise and nondemeaning, helpful criticism.

- Take part of the blame.

- Are enthusiastic.

- Have strong personal power.

- Never criticize one team member to another team member.

- Look out for their team members.

- Are good listeners.

- Make clear assignments of duties but encourage input outside of specific job area.

- May not always implement suggestions, but always encourage them.

- Empower team members.

- Have the ability to evaluate, react to, and defuse crises calmly.

● Both team members and the team leader are loyal to the team.

● See Brainstorming; Hiring; Project Management.

Telephone Tips

The telephone can be your best business friend or your worst time management enemy.

- First identify yourself.
- Smile while you're talking.
- Place your own calls.
- Get to the point.
- Don't use a speakerphone without permission.
- Return all calls the same business day or apologize for your tardiness.
- As much as possible, answer your own phone. Depending on your business and for time management purposes, you may want to have your calls screened.
- Picture the person you're talking to.
- Minimize phone tag by:
    - Returning calls at a specific time of day (bunch your interruptions). The recom-

mended time is just before lunch or the end of the day. People are more likely to be at their desks and more likely to be brief and to the point at these times.

- Leaving a message with more than just your name. Include topic/purpose so the return caller will be prepared.

- Call your own number periodically to see how and how quickly your phone is being answered.

- Reduce phone time by starting with "I've only got a minute but I knew your call was important and I wanted to get back to you."

- See Listening.

Time-Saving Tips

Don't major in the minors.

● Do it right the first time.

● Decide which tasks you need to do an "A" effort on and which tasks need only a "B" effort.

● Discipline yourself to cut down on nonbusiness talk and socializing.

● Keep one task on your desk at a time.

● Take the last half hour of the day to organize your desk and plan for the next day.

● Take something to read while you wait.

● Leave detailed phone messages so that a response isn't always required.

● Delegate when possible.

● When appropriate, make a phone call instead of writing a memo or letter.

● Start the day with a prioritized "TO DO" list. A good example is:

Must <u>DO</u> today.	Must <u>CALL</u> today.
<u>DO</u> if time allows.	<u>CALL</u> if time allows.

● Set deadlines.

● Use car time as think time.

● Handle paper only once.

● Use time-saving devices:

   ● Buy a good time management calendar system, such as Franklin, Filofax, or Daytimer.

   ● Become computer literate and use your computer.

   ● Consider buying a car phone.

   ● Consider adding voice mail to your telephones.

● See Open Door Policy; Telephone Tips.

Time Thieves

Time you waste is gone forever.

- Being too detail oriented or more detail oriented than the company norm.

- Majoring in the minors.

- Catching hot-potato problems—that is, catching problems your employees throw at you and taking charge when they are stuck. Give employees a few ideas on how to deal with the issue and then throw the hot potato back to them to solve.

- Getting behind on the paper influx. Sort each morning into:

  - To do today.

  - To do ASAP.

  - Later.

  - Trash or stash. (If you have trouble throwing it away, stash it.)

151

- Not delegating.
- Waiting.
- Unnecessary conversations.

- See Time-Saving Tips.

Total Quality Management

To be the very best.

- TQM (Total Quality Management) is an evolving management philosophy based on the following components:
- Total:
  - Refers to involvement and empowerment of all employees.
  - Cross-functional and cross-departmental teams are used to assess and improve processes.
  - Total external and internal customer focus.
  - Value added in the eyes of the customer.
  - System is totally data driven.
- Quality:
  - Meeting or exceeding customers' expectations.
  - Doing it right the first time.

- Continuing evaluation and improvement.

- Focusing only on activities that add value to the customer and eliminating nonvalue-added activities.

● Management:

- Top management is committed to TQM and understands that management-driven systems, not the individuals, are the problems.

- Focuses on How can we fix the system? not Whom can we blame?

- Uses the Plan, Do, Check, Correct system.

- Commits to ongoing training and education.

- Prioritizes all objectives and goals in terms of quality and customer focus.

● The primary goal of TQM is to increase long-term profits by increasing quality, increasing customer focus, and decreasing costs.

● See Customer Service; Suggested Reading (Crosby).

Traits of a Good Employee

A good employee always makes the boss look good.

● A good employee:

  ● Is loyal and committed.

  ● Always attempts to see things from the company's point of view.

  ● Shares company goals and priorities.

  ● Is flexible.

  ● Is dependable; when assigned a responsibility, no one has to double check to make sure it's completed.

  ● Doesn't hide problems.

  ● Adapts to the boss's style.

  ● Takes initiative and follows through.

  ● Is self-motivated.

  ● Knows when to ask for help.

- Along with voicing complaints, presents solutions.

- Is a team player.

- Maintains a positive attitude.

- Has good self-esteem.

● See Getting Along with Your Boss.

Unions

The us-versus-them mentality is a thing of the past.

- Know exactly how your company's contract (collective bargaining agreement) with the union reads. If you don't know, ask someone who does.

- Be familiar with all union policies and regulations.

- Deal openly and honestly with the union.

- Be clear on what issues you should handle and what issues should be referred to the union steward.

- Maintain a good relationship with the union steward. Keep the steward informed.

- Attempt to resolve small complaints before they become grievances.

● Never try to block a grievance.

● Remember, the union is just as invested in the success of the company as management is.

● See Conflict Resolution.

Acknowledgments

Harvey Mackay for, unbeknownst to him, giving us tremendous inspiration.

Adrienne Hickey for her kindness to us.

Stephanie Laidman for believing in *The Brass Tacks Manager* and having the courage to go for forgiveness instead of permission.

Bruce Tracy for his speeding bullet style and for making it fun.

For information on speaking and training by the authors contact:

On Target Training
3520 West 75th Street, Suite 201
Prairie Village, KS 66208

ABOUT THE AUTHORS

Pat Kaufman began her career as a psychotherapist and developed her expertise and interest in business as she became increasingly aware that many of her clients' problems centered on managing the personal/family/work balance. Still maintaining an active private psychotherapy practice, she also acts as a management consultant, focusing on beginning entrepreneurs and small or family businesses. Her clients have also included Fortune 500 companies. A popular speaker, she lives with her husband and two children in Prairie Village, Kansas.

Cindy Wetmore is the Director of Retail Training and Services and a project leader in the sales and marketing division of Hallmark Cards, Inc. Her experience also includes two years as an independent contractor for National Seminars, Inc., a public-seminar company, where she presented over 150 seminars throughout the United States and Canada. Continual requests from seminar attendees for concise, practical, how-to desk reference material led her to develop the idea for a book like *The Brass Tacks Manager*. Married and a stepmother of two, she lives in Lake Quivira, Kansas.